HOW TO WRITE FAST

SEAN M. PLATT
NEEVE SILVER

INTRODUCTION

In the past ten years I've written every kind of copy.

SEO articles, freelance everything, sales letters, email autoresponders, web copy, educational content — both ghostwritten and with my name on it — options, scripts, and over two-hundred fiction and nonfiction books. I have generated many millions of dollars with my words.

Our profession draws a direct line between speed and income.

The more I write the more I make. But I'm unwilling to sacrifice quality. I care more about my name than my revenue. The strength of the Sterling & Stone story studio rests in the excellence of our storytelling, and that can never acquiesce to speed.

We go as fast as we can until we can't go faster, but never faster than we should be going at any given time.

The optimum speed differs for every storyteller in our studio, but writing *fast for you* is the Sterling & Stone way. And by the time you finish this book, I hope you'll make it *your* way, too.

There is no universal metric for defining the speed of fast writing. Growth is relative to where you are and where you can be. In the last year, Dave has gone from an average of just under five-hundred words per day to just over twenty-two hundred, more than a four-hundred percent increase. That number is still continuing to climb. Even better, Dave is now getting four times the number of words in less time, so now he can take off weekends, which helps him recharge.

One-hundred percent of our storytellers have found that writing significantly faster than they did not only helps them to tell more stories in less time, but substantial growth as a writer is a natural result. This is automatic, but only if you are paying attention as you go.

As you learn to write faster, you learn to write better. But only if you do it consciously.

Writing fast allows you to switch off your internal editor and *just write.* This makes it easier to tap into your bigger ideas and achieve a clearer level of articulation. Better writing and more inspirational moments.

Writing fast makes writing what it should be — an almost magical process where you tap into your creative mind to communicate ideas like instincts.

Switching off your internal editor is hard, especially at first. But if you've been believing the lie that it's impossible, knock it off now. Getting out of your own way is the essential element to writing fast.

Nothing else will have a greater impact on your ability to achieve and maintain your optimal speed.

You must believe you can do this. More importantly, you must believe it isn't even a big deal — it's no more than a result of your intentions and effort. But more than that, you must believe in the value of changing your behavior. *Wanting to write faster* won't lead to a lasting change. You need to understand why you should be writing fast in the first place, agree with the premise, and use it to evolve the patterns in your life.

Writing faster starts in the mind. The act comes entirely from signals in your brain, so shifting how it operates while writing is the best way to evolve your speed. It's a change in how you think about and approach your craft. So instead of giving you limbering exercises to increase your finger speed, we'll teach you how to retrain your mind, let go of the obstacles holding you back, and unleash your inner speed.

————

There's a lot to absorb here, and we want to make it as easy as we can. Knowledge leads to insight, but we want that path to be straightforward and confusion-free. So, a note of clarification to get things started.

Who wrote this?

You saw two names on the cover this book: *Sean M. Platt* and *Neeve Silver.*

We're the co-authors. *Nice to meet you.*

But instead of saying "we" throughout the entire book and risking sounding like the Queen of England, or jumping back and forth between our perspectives so much that your head spins, we're going to go ahead and say "I" — meaning Sean, since I (Sean) am currently writing the rough draft.

Neeve will just jump in with her amazing

insights and make me sound way better than I would otherwise. She wrote that last sentence. I'm sure you can see how confusing it would be if we had to keep stopping to tell you who was writing what.

Who are those other people?

You'll hear mention of a whole host of other storytellers throughout this book. We'll mention Johnny and Dave, my podcast co-hosts and long-time co-writers. But you'll also meet Ninie, Marie, Joel and many others. No, they aren't caricatures I invented to make up examples. These are the remarkable storytellers who I'm sure aren't all that different from you, except they're crazy enough to write with us here at Sterling & Stone.

Our studio is comprised of around twenty story-tellers who share worlds, ideas, laughter, and a lot of hacks for improving our craft and going collectively faster. They make me a better storyteller daily, and I couldn't write this book without including their examples and helpful tips. Whenever I say "we" in this book, I'm referring to the studio as a whole. Anytime I mention someone who is not me, Neeve, Johnny, or Dave, they are another storyteller from our studio.

Momentum

But wait, there's more! This book is just the beginning of learning to write fast. It's only one section of four from our larger compilation, *Momentum* (which, depending on when you're reading this book, is coming soon or already available). *Momentum* will fill in all the details to help you not just write faster, but maintain consistent speed over the long haul. It's about producing work you love at a pace that will make you a better, more successful storyteller for the rest of your life.

So why the shorter book? Because I know if you want to write fast, you value TIME. This is the quickest way to inject the info you need into your brain to start writing faster.

If you want to put what you learn in this book into practice, then pick up *Momentum* and begin to establish the habits that will help you build and maintain a better writing speed for the rest of your life.

———

Speaking of putting what you learn into practice, we've created a *60-Second Summary* of the key points in this book for you to print and keep handy as you begin to incorporate what you learned.

You'll find the summary, PLUS all our extra downloadable goodies for the entire Stone Tablet range in our **Extras Vault.**

Visit **SterlingAndStone.net/Extras** to get access.

DISCLAIMER

Before I show you how to write faster, we need to make sure we're totally on the same page.

Writing fast takes practice.

If we do our job with this book, you're going to be incrementally faster as soon as you finish it. Then, if you keep working hard and smart, you'll get faster and faster while also improving the quality of your work. Eventually, your writing muscles will be strong enough to carry higher word counts than you ever thought possible.

But it absolutely will not be easy.

Our studio is stuffed with storytellers who can boast more than a million words a year. But only one of them came to us that way. All the others were born through internal iteration. Many of our writers were writing haphazardly, like you might be right now. They might have days where they hit a few thousand words, but they were only doing it once a month or so, if they were lucky. Some were barely writing at all before joining our studio, even though they were serious about their dreams. Now they are moving forward consistently and every one of them has increased their speed and their word counts.

Our results aren't typical, but they are possible. This is what we do full-time. Some of us have already clocked in our ten-thousand hours of practice. Shared craftsmanship abounds, and that makes going faster more of a natural lifestyle.

We want to share our most effective habits with you. Read it all, pick the ones that feel most suited to you and your situation, then design a new strategy around them. Try it out, tweak as you go, and you'll constantly improve.

Yes, we want you to write faster, but we also want you to write *happier.* That's the point. The goal is not to become a word machine; it's to make writing a pleasure so the words come as easily as the actions behind anything else you're dying to do.

Understand, you don't have to be AMAZING here, you just need to be a little better than you were the last time, then do that over and over and over again. This is the cumulative interest of writing. The Eighth Wonder of the World. Figure out your personal formula for high-quality writing at an accelerated pace and it becomes significantly easier to build a business around your craft.

This book would not have been possible without constant evolution.

I learned to write dead skin of the Internet (SEO articles) as fast as I could because I made five bones per finished piece and needed as many as I could to buy food for my family. 10K-word days were born.

Today that's called *making cheese* — more on that later.

Once I could hit 10K a day producing garbage I wasn't proud of, I learned to write sales copy that paid ten times what I was making per word to start, and eventually more than a hundred times by the time I was clocking out of copywriting and moving into full-time fiction.

It's a lot harder to butter your bread when no one is offering either one to you. I quit a lucrative gig to gamble on being a full-time storyteller, so my words mattered more than ever.

I learned to do everything in this book so I could feed both of my families — the one at home and the one made up of the storytellers at Sterling & Stone.

I could crank out ten-thousand words a day of crappy SEO copy a decade ago, but I couldn't have done a quarter that number of high-quality fiction words. Not even close.

Now I can. This book will tell you how.

You're different from me and everyone in the studio, but you're also the same. Pay attention and look for the things that resonate most, then use them to change the way you write forever.

There is no EZ-Button. The best way to get better is to write no less than five days a week and constantly improve. The worst way is to believe you can dabble your way into brilliance.

PART I

WHY WRITE FAST

1

WHY WRITE FAST

Times have changed.

Not too long from now, no one will blink at how quickly some outliers are currently writing.

The craft has come a long way. I'm only an author because of the speed with which I can approach both the business and art. If I was on a manual typewriter with paper and ribbon, there's no way I would know the pure joy of bouncing from story to story that keeps me getting out of the bed without an alarm each and every morning.

Even after we had computers, publishers still only had so much bandwidth to market their product. Bookstores only had so much shelf space. The Internet fired the first shot at the paradigm, but the

Kindle took a Gatling gun to the way things used to be done.

Writing fast isn't about hitting the algorithms, achieving "rapid release," or even getting more assets on the market, even though all those things will be easier once you write faster. This is all about improving your craft. One book at a time. The faster you go, the better you get. (You might not believe this yet, but by the end of this book, you will.)

Shelf space is now infinite and everyone has a voice. So, make yours move faster and stay sharper. Demand more of your abilities. Even if you can only see them a little, they are in there a lot.

The old way made sense, but only in the same way it made sense to wait for a connection on dialup before broadband became a possibility. Authors used to work on one book a year, constantly massaging it to make it better and better. In Sterling & Stone, and in the larger indie publishing community, none of us could do that out of necessity. Fiction has been our full-time jobs for a while now, so we needed to treat our stories with some of the same business-minded respect we gave our freelance writing. We could never afford to take our time or go over anything over and over and over. At least not leisurely.

Everything we produce has multiple passes, but we're never reading them while sipping wine by the fireplace.

Instead, we choose to write ten or more books a year and take a grand leap forward in our abilities. Our projects now are much more ambitious and complicated than they were, or even could have been, when we started out.

The process of writing fast and consistent made that possible more than any inherent talent, and that's true for every storyteller in our swiftly moving stable.

We're all waging the same war for time. We all long for more minutes in the day that will never be ours no matter how much we want them or even how much we're willing to pay. Hours are truly finite, and yet born raconteurs want to tell as many stories as they can. We currently have five fiction imprints and a ravenous fanbase for our nonfiction books. We want to satisfy our muses and feel fulfilled creatively while also building our assets and brand. It hurts to put stories we can't wait to write on the back burner and see zero reasons to move any slower than our abilities will allow.

Sometimes we go so fast that we trip and break our stories. Those occasions require extra work.

That's fine; we still end up ahead ... and smarter about story than we were a book ago.

Quality and speed are threaded together. Implement what you learn in this book and your growth as a writer will accelerate alongside your overall pace. Painters who paint are always improving, chefs who are constantly cooking are bound to develop better recipes, and carpenters who spend all their time in the workshop tend to have the most impressive woodworking.

You're also better when you get out of your own way, and writing fast helps you remove the filter. Writing is treated differently from these other disciplines for no intelligent reason. Many writers think the best way to improve their work is to sit and think about it.

This is completely wrong.

Humans learn by doing. And good writing doesn't come from the analytical mind. Like anything else, it comes from practicing, seeing what you can improve, and then doing it again. So, outsmart conventional thinking and teach yourself to do things better today than yesterday.

Let's start by knocking out a few of the reasons writers think they shouldn't write fast.

2

REASONS WRITERS DON'T WANT TO WRITE FAST

SOME OF THE resistance to writing fast is perfectly understandable. Some of it is silly. All of it can be placed into the proper containers of thought and stowed somewhere out of the way to keep them from disturbing you.

A slow timeline is like a security blanket. But really, it's just a great example of Parkinson's Law: *Work expands so as to fill the time available for its completion.*

If you give yourself a year to finish a book, you'll spend a year on the draft. But if you give yourself a month, you can do that, too. Even if you can't, you might be able to do it in two. And the book that took a year probably isn't six times better.

Bend the math in your favor. Believe in yourself more than you do.

That's where a lot of writers break. Right there in the beginning, doubting their ideas instead of giving them a chance, working the weak ideas to make them stronger.

We all handle our ideas differently. Some of us like to talk them out, others like to create a timeline. We might use a 40-Sentence outline to flesh out our ideas, bring them to one of our story rooms for some general discussion, or pound out a page or ten of free writing to figure out what our characters are trying to say. But everyone has a process to distill their ideas and keep them from the curse of not being excited about their stories.

Lack of excitement will slow you down more than just about anything else.

Doubt about your ideas is a drag, for sure. But a lack of enthusiasm turns writing into work, and that's a virtual guarantee your project will stall. Even if you're good at cranking out words when you're not feeling it, that's a difficult thing to sustain. It's also the opposite of living the dream.

These two are related. Doubt your ideas and your enthusiasm for the story will wane. Once that happens, every paragraph will be a struggle, and speed suddenly feels like an impossible achievement.

Writing faster helps you close the door on your doubt. You want to hold that enthusiasm and let it carry you through your work. If you're used to doubting everything, this will take practice.

Another rationale, reckless in its reasoning, is the longer a writer takes, the better the work will be. We brushed against this already, but let's take another moment to talk about how truly ridiculous it is, and how the opposite can also be a danger.

The longer you spend on something, the worse you might be making it.

While trying to avoid sounding like an amateur, an author might go over a work so many times that it becomes overwritten and stripped of immediacy, its original soul picked over like bones on a bird in the desert.

At Sterling & Stone, we have a saying for the first four drafts of your novel: Say it, say what you mean, say it well, then spit and shine before sending it off to the editor.

Aim for four highly focused passes, three once you're an ace at it, always understanding that regardless of the ultimate number of revisions, the first one should always come fast because slow drafts are often more tentative. They are borne from your over-thinking logical mind instead of the place where your true storytelling genius lies — your subconscious.

Fear comes in many forms. Every one of them holds you back, preventing your best efforts by telling you what you can't do instead of inspiring you to take a chance and see what might happen. Dave thought about writing a book for years. Ever since high school. But he had gray in his beard before he published his first book, and that was only after I had spent three years nagging him about it.

Maybe you've tried before and only managed to produce drivel. So what? Michael Jordan didn't even start on his high school basketball team. Dr. Seuss was rejected by twenty-seven publishers, and Stephen King beat him by three with an even thirty. I just finished reading a biography on Walt Disney. Spoiler alert: *the guy failed a lot.*

We all stumble. My first book is garbage. But because I finished it, I knew I could write another one. Practice makes perfect, but you can't be unwilling to practice for fear it won't be good enough immediately or it will take too long before it is.

The book I just finished before starting this one has both a restrained sprawl and a level of thematic depth I wouldn't have even attempted a few years ago. I certainly wouldn't have believed I could've written a story like that for five-thousand words or so each day throughout the project's entire runtime.

But that's what this book is for. It's supposed to change you.

If you're one of those writers who has a hard time seeing the end, and that's keeping you from a sustainable writing habit or slowing you down when it should be story time, then it's time to change the way you approach your discipline.

Getting to the end is now your job. Second guessing yourself is getting in the way of your performance.

Write is rewriting, so keep the story moving forward, knowing you'll need to add and subtract throughout your next pass. Don't allow yourself to get lost in the weeds, fretting about where it will all go. That will only dilute your results before you've achieved them.

The math is in your favor. Take all the reasons

you think you can't write fast and put them behind you.

If you continue to write incrementally faster, then you will constantly be writing faster than you ever have before. And eventually, faster than you ever thought possible.

3
———

WHY YOU CAN WRITE FASTER THAN
YOU THINK

IF YOU THINK you can't write much faster than you already do, you're absolutely correct.

If you're sure you can, then you're also totally right.

So, let's start by changing the way you think.

Maybe you're aware of what's possible, but you're reading this book more as a curiosity than anything else. To see how *they* do it. Because according to the story you've been telling yourself for a while, there's no way *you* could ever do that.

But that's a lie. Even if you will never be able to run a four-minute mile, you can absolutely train yourself to run faster than you do right now. Writing is the same thing.

We've seen it countless times in the last ten

years. Not only among all the storytellers we're working with right now in the studio, but with hundreds of authors in our audience who have told us how much our example has meant to them.

It all started with Johnny. He was the everyman when our studio got started. Writers in our audience related to him because he had spent a dozen years on his first book. But he's an optimizer, and there was no way he was going to let a chance to turn fiction into a business pass him by. If Johnny needed to increase his speed by a factor of ten, then dammit, that was exactly what he was going to do.

The first couple of years we were writing together, Johnny was producing 1.5 million words of high-quality rough draft fiction. More than enough to build a business around. Writing a million words or more per year isn't for everyone, but our story-tellers keep raising their hands one at a time, signing up for 1M word commitments.

It's 2,740 words a day. Without systems, that's nearly impossible to sustain. With systems, it's part of your life.

Eileen is our latest to raise her hand. She's written all her life but before joining our studio, she didn't have discipline and could produce around one book a year. Eileen is exactly the sort of storyteller we love. Full of voice and eager to learn. She's funny and loud, drunk or sober. She's highly creative and willing to work hard. She's picking up new disciplines all the time and just last week committed to a million words for next year.

But that wasn't the biggest surprise.

Dave made the same commitment.

You might have some idea how crazy that is, but in case you don't, I really need to tell you.

Dave is our resident over-thinker and general grumpy bear. We've been writing together for ten years. In that time, his average book count per year was around three books. Five was his peak, and that nearly ruined him. And some of the words in those books were written by me. Before Dave adopted some of these philosophies, he maxed out at around a quarter of a million words in his very best year.

Not only has Dave's average word count already dramatically increased, he's going to ratchet up again, and — this is a much bigger deal for Dave — make the year-long commitment.

That's unprecedented and only possible because of everything you are reading right now.

Writing is simple communication. If you're going slow, it's probably at least in part because you're overthinking it. Most of us don't edit every sentence out of our mouth. Those who do can come off as neurotic or worse. We can all see this in speech, but many people fail to recognize how evident it is in writing.

If you don't self-edit when you speak, then you shouldn't do it in the raw drafts of your writing. At least not if speed is the muscle you're working to build.

Worrying you'll write something inferior is silly. Truth is, you will tap into your natural voice and write better copy in less time. The more you do it, the truer that statement will be.

Your mind will always move faster than your hands. If you're aptly prepared (both mentally and by knowing your story before you start), able to focus for a sustained period of time, and can stay ahead of your lower self that loves to dabble in self-sabotage, you will find your flow.

Because I empowered myself with this freedom, the times I have written the fastest — not just hammering the page with words but laying them down with intention, like a road without angles for my reader to race down, leaving the elegant bends to the narrative itself — have produced some of my very best work.

This is true for every storyteller I've ever collaborated with.

I have the most experience with Dave and Johnny. When either one of them is under duress during a draft, it always shows up in their work. There is a direct correlation between quality and speed, but not the way most people believe. Often the longer you take, the lower the quality.

So, stop making excuses. It's hard to write fast and well, but it's a skill at which you can constantly improve. You've already committed to wanting this or you wouldn't have bought this book. You wouldn't be reading it now. Doing anything less than your best from this moment forward means leaving your dreams on the table.

But also, really consider the following before you go forward.

Do you really WANT to write faster?

That's a question worth serious consideration. We agree you're committed, and I know you can do it. But do you *want to*, or is this something you think you *should do* to be successful?

Huge difference.

The irony is, if you're only doing it to be successful, you probably never will be.

If you think writing is hard or see the art as laborious, none of this is going to change that and your mindset will absolutely stand in your way. If you see writing as a joy and want more of that in your life because you have stories to tell and are looking for ways to tell them faster, then a great change is ahead of you.

You can only turn the crank for so long before it stops working, but learning to love what you do will give your art perpetual motion.

Most of this is a decision. Simply *deciding* to write faster. It won't happen overnight, but neither will losing twenty pounds or lifting a hundred, being able to run for distance or speed, learning a language or playing an instrument. Skills take time to develop. This is one of the most valuable ones you will ever have. Treat it with reverence.

Decide it can be done, then do it.

Here's what will happen.

4

IF YOU WRITE FASTER

WHETHER YOU'RE WRITING for love or money, ideas are your currency.

You want a factory full of them that never stops producing? Learn to write faster. We are never looking for good ideas and probably never will be again. Because they happen every day as part of doing business. We already have more ideas and concepts than we could ever produce, and the gap is constantly widening. The more we write, the more they come to us. It's a broken faucet with the nearest plumber two counties down. This state can only exist after all the years of writing fast. *Every day.*

Learn to write fast and your story will start to feel like it's writing itself.

Story itself will become a character in your life. A best friend you become phenomenal at talking to. Someone you get to know better with every conversation and who helps you to know more about yourself.

I used to pay much more attention to the words than the story, so they always came slower. But every time I told a different story, I got better at telling my tales overall. Speed leads to exposure and experience. Any writer paying attention through all of that will develop a sharper instinct.

Ninie is seventy-two years young and a lifetime writer. She was a journalist before writing fiction, and you can read it in her gorgeous southern-soaked voice. She wrote fifteen books before coming to us, all almost exactly a hundred-thousand words. She doesn't know if she's capable of writing any other length and says, "They just come out that way."

Ninie will write and publish more words in the next two years than she has in all the time before that.

No dip in quality, but a dramatic escalation in enjoyment. She's never had more fun writing. Part of that is the studio itself. Ninie recently said she didn't even know how lonely she had been until she had something to compare. Now she's much happier working around so many other creative minds..

That's worth mentioning because collaboration can super-boost your speed. We all go faster because we have each other. Collaboration is a giant topic, but it can be another powerful tool in your personal studio, and it's the one that makes ours work as well as it does.

Ninie keeps having new record days and posting them in our accountability channel. We can all imagine her laughing in triumph as she enters her freshest winning number.

Speed is especially important to Ninie. We were asking our authors what each of them wanted, and high on Ninie's list was *legacy*. When we were talking about five-year goals for each of us, she said, "You all are so young. Five years doesn't mean the same thing to me as it does to all of you."

We all appreciate these lessons, but Ninie feels them more deeply than the rest of us.

I want you to appreciate them like all of us, feel them like Ninie, and work harder than you ever have to change the way you approach your writing.

Because yes, you will create a bigger and better legacy in less time. If writing is your business, you want to grow your audience and stack your abilities as fast as you possibly can.

Let's start by building a foundation to make writing less about grinding through the words and more about sitting down to tell a story you can't wait to tell.

PART II

FOUNDATIONS FOR SPEED

5
———

THE PLAN

THE BETTER YOU PLAN, the faster you write.

We have a whole section on planning in the full *Momentum* book, but for now, understand this is the blood that will keep your speed pumping. The better you plan, the more you'll be prepared to know and tell your story. This doesn't mean you have to be a plotter to write fast, but it does mean the more familiar you are with the material and the more you have carefully thought it all out, the faster it will flow.

Planning is separate from writing fast. One skill precedes the other. Learn to wax on and off before you start throwing punches. Let's quickly cover the basics you need to write faster.

First, you need to have a skeleton of your story

with a basic structure in place, all parts of the outline accessible, and a deep enough under-standing of what happens in the narrative that you could tell a reasonably coherent version of your story to someone sitting next to you at party, even after you've had a couple of drinks.

You can be a full-blown outliner or someone who likes to see how the story will unfold from beat to beat and chapter to chapter, but everyone needs a framework to keep them aligned with the story.

I prefer fully fleshed-out beats for most things I write because the constant prompts keep my fingers moving along with my mind. But I can also easily adapt and write a scene with only a few basic bullet points if I need to. No matter what, I need some sort of structure to act as my compass, to ensure I know where I'm going and that I'm taking my characters on an actual journey instead of meandering from one errant idea to the next.

One way to look at planning is separating out the deciding from the doing. Your mind is a machine; it works best when it's focused on one thing or in one mode.

Planning is making the big decisions about the story. Who the characters are, what kind of story it is, what you are trying to say, and what main events in the story you most want to hit.

Writing is letting the story flow out of you onto the page. It's the doing, the actual telling of the story.

Nothing will slow you down more than shifting modes. If you have to stop every few paragraphs to decide what will happen next, then you are literally changing which part of your brain you're using. This will impede any chance you have at flow in your story.

It doesn't mean you can't pants if that's what you love to do. But understand the process and know that excellent pantsing comes from letting the details find you while you're in a flow state. You still know where you're trying to go. You still have already made the big decisions. Anything you can decide in advance that doesn't remove your enjoyment of the writing process *should be decided.* Never make your brain shift out of writing mode for decision-making or critiquing (more on this later) unless it's absolutely necessary.

The key to writing fast isn't having to think whether to write or what to write, it's just doing it. If you have a structure and know you're planning for the next scene, it will come faster once you arrive.

The art of writing is essentially the art of decision-making. Every book is comprised of several thousand choices all stitched together to make a single story. Lubricate your decisions and you also dim the resistance, making the act of composing that much easier to execute.

You already have to decide on the story, structure, characters, and scenes, not to mention all the little details — what things look like, what room your characters are in, how they look and move and behave.

Quality writing requires specificity. Your reader needs enough details to give your story texture and help your audience create the mental imagery they need to feel like they are a part of your narrative.

But every decision takes energy, and probably more than you're giving them credit for. Instead of having to invent every single thing, you can use visual shortcuts to inject a dose of texture and reality into your work. Cast your characters to make it easier to visualize expression and movement. You want people, not stick figures, and using an actor as a starting point will get you going without over-thinking or second guessing yourself too much. Know the locations you're going to write about ahead of time. Make a folder from your online photo safari or get outside with your camera. Live to color your story.

Even if you are writing in an epic fantasy world conceived entirely in your imagination, landing on a real detail your reader can cling to will help them imagine your story and bring your writing to life.

If you want to write fast, then you'll also need to get comfortable writing around what you don't know. This might be the biggest creative conflict Dave and I have ever wrestled our way through. Right now, we're not yet where we ultimately want to go, but we have a solution that's made it the best things have ever been for us.

Never forget you are the director of your story, which means even if you're not writing a screenplay, you still get to control where the camera is centered. If you don't want your reader to see something, then make sure to obscure it. Dave would never make a character a neurosurgeon because he doesn't know a thing about neurosurgery. I can't imagine a more limiting restriction. Our regular argument goes something like this.

"What if the guy is a neurosurgeon?"

"No," Dave says.

"Why not?"

"I don't know anything about that."

"So, don't put him in surgery."

And Dave will protest. "I won't know how he thinks."

"Like a human," I'll remind him. "It's a scientific fact that neurosurgeons are humans, too."

The solution to this problem is now I change the professions on anything I'm writing as a rough draft, while Dave sticks to his cops, artists, journalists, abused children, and school teachers.

But he is right about one thing: when it comes to going *fast,* writing around what you don't know is a time-honored shortcut. Done well, it's something the reader will never notice. Done poorly, it will ruin their experience. This is a tic that tends to get more evident by the book, so get control of it early.

If there's something you should have a basic understanding of before starting your story, it makes sense to familiarize yourself with it now in the planning stage. You'll write faster without having to slow down during the narrative, and you'll know your world that much better.

Research doesn't always mean what people think it means. I research a lot, but it comes in the form of watching movies for mood and maybe some tidbits to use, reading books for tone, fact-checking after a scene is written to enhance it. The latent, by-the-way "research" that occurs when you're simply familiar with something.

I constantly draw from the surface of my life. Conversations, things on my mind, the unresolved minutia of my day. Things I watched the night before or was maybe thinking about while waking up. You may think this is too obvious, but done well, it's the opposite. It will make your stories feel real and immediate, and when you read that part of your book back later, you'll feel a warm tickle of nostalgia as you remember where you were and what you were feeling when you wrote it. And sometimes that's the best of what this craft can give us.

I recently went through some harrowing shit with my parents, and it infected every part of my creative life for a while. That yielded some wonderful ideas. It could have been a disaster and slowed my momentum to nothing. Instead, I turned that energy into a positive force, and my productivity went up rather than down.

When you get to the end of each day, don't stop. Look at the next scene, whatever you're going to start with tomorrow. Study the beats or outline. Memorize them if possible. Let them play in your head as you go about your day. Give enough mind to this and you'll be so comfortable with the story, your words will just *flow*. Then there will be a minimum of unnecessary decisions to make. Your subconscious will deliver the story to you.

Planning is a shortcut. Give your story an outline or skeleton so you know the bigger things; collect the details and texture in your life to color your story with the brush of reality.

You're armed with enough of a plan to get started. Now you need a system.

6

WHY YOU NEED A SYSTEM

A SYSTEM IS NON-NEGOTIABLE.

The smarter your systems, the tighter your possible flow.

This is because the right system will build a bridge between your talent and your skill. Most writers wrongly believe their performance at the keyboard is reflective of their innate ability to think fast and move their fingers in harmony with that thought. In reality, a storyteller can improve any part of their process once practice drives their goals.

If you want to be the best, or at least significantly better than you are, then you need to have a seed of talent to water, but it never needs to be anything more than that.

Many writers wait for inspiration to strike, or

worse, to "feel" like writing. They think they will write better when in the proper headspace. But that's harder to find if it's not a place you cultivate. A system that fosters consistent practice will make it a place you regularly return to.

Believe you can build the right system to support you, then work hard to feed your natural talent.

Improving most skills — like playing the piano, shooting free throws, or running long-distance — is a straightforward process. People working to get better at any one of those disciplines would know exactly what to do.

But storytelling is different.

We don't approach this craft with the same expectations, and there is so much more curiosity around purely creative endeavors. Playing the piano is different from composing music to be played on. There is an unnecessary reverence placed on the act of writing that is likely holding you back from going as fast as your brain is capable of going. Even the most naturally talented among us can wrongly believe their talent will run dry and they must preserve the levels in whatever reservoir they have, which usually means going at a slower, more comfortable pace.

All of that is wrong.

There is a much better way. Enhance your ability to create by developing a system to support you.

Cindy loves to cook, which makes me damn lucky. She would never call herself a chef because the word is grandiose for what she does: using her soul to feed her family each day. She's traveled the world and still cooks much of our food using an ancient wok that's seen more than its share of Asia. Cindy's love of the discipline, her natural talent, and many decades of practice have made it so cooking is sometimes as simple as opening the fridge and getting started.

However, this is never her preferred way to cook.

Yes, Cindy can make something delicious on the fly. But doing it that way every day would drive her nuts. The quality of our meals would go down, she would spend more time and money on the food, her enjoyment would be diluted, and none of us would be as happy. Instead, Cindy has systems for everything from shopping to preparing her ingredients to rotating flavors and interests. Most of this is invisible and never discussed or even thought much about. She doesn't think about her systems because they are an ingrained part of the way she works and mostly only noticeable when it breaks or goes missing. Only then does Cindy realize how dependent she's become on her personal flow.

This is why you need a system. Even if you *can* make things up as you go along, that's not a positive process. Working on the fly usually leads to lost time, even if you believe it's doing the opposite.

Don't worry about having the perfect system. It won't be. The goal isn't perfection; it's to improve as you go and understand yourself better throughout the process.

A system lets you fly. The right organizational structure won't restrain or box you in. Rather, it will give you the wings to soar.

I can talk a bit about my system and how it's evolved over time. I can also give you some examples from our studio that prove creativity and great ideas both stem from speed. But I can't develop your system for you. I can't even do that for any of our storytellers, and I work with them every day.

My system isn't your system.

Your system will be born from your intentions, effort, and iteration.

After many years and all the mistakes and measurements that get packed into the months, I now rarely ever write in the evening. I'll work after dinner, no problem, but I should never be writing then because I will produce work that's maybe half as good in twice the time.

I've trained myself to start writing shortly after I wake up because that's the time of day when my brain is moving fastest and I've not yet diluted my willpower. Writing, or creating something from nothing, is the most difficult thing I do each day. Whether that's working on an outline for a new story or getting fresh words into my latest draft, creating characters, conflict, or narrative out of the blue is more taxing on my mind than anything else. The cognitive load is fun but heavy, so it makes sense that I'd want to focus on it while I'm fresh.

I always prefer to do my most difficult tasks first, and training myself to finish them in the morning helped to make me consistently productive. Now that writing is my most important task, my system demands I start with it.

Most of the reasoning for getting my words in early is that I'm teaching myself what kind of creator I am — the kind who gets up every day and gets his words in early. The more I do this, the easier it is to repeat the behavior. We'll talk about streaks and patterns and other ways to mentally hack yourself in *Momentum*, but for now it's important that you understand your behavior will set a precedent here just like it does in other parts of your life.

If you're someone who snacks throughout the day, then you're more likely to gain a few pounds a year. If, on the other hand, you're the type of person who takes walks throughout the day, extra pounds won't be a problem. Decide who you want to be.

Beyond living up to the standard I've set for myself, I also understand how truly limited willpower is as a resource. Decision fatigue is a real thing. It happens when our lack of energy or focus leads us to poor decisions. As a storyteller, the quality of your choices is everything. Wrong decisions in your draft lead to additional work in the revision. Writing while you're fresh helps to curb those issues. The more decisions you make, the worse you get at weighing your options until you reset — maybe after some Netflix and a good night's sleep.

The last and perhaps most significant reason I write first thing is because it helps me gain momentum, which is the essential element in using my writing speed to fuel the rest of my day. When I've had a good morning writing, everything else in my day usually falls right into place.

A typical writing day starts with me waking up

before the alarm, making my coffee, then taking the mug into my office. Ideally, I don't check Slack, social media, email or anything else, because I know it's a distraction that will send my mind somewhere away from the story I'm trying to tell. In truth, I'm weaker here than I want to be and often lose a half-hour or so before I actually get down to it. This is silly, and on those occasions when I outsmart my worst tendencies, the superior results always speak for themselves.

My workdays are divided into three parts. Maker Time, Me Time, and Manager Time.

Maker Time is when I write, and it runs from the time I get started in the morning to noon. I write in sprints and take short breaks to walk in between them. For best results, I'm doing deep work during this time, which means I don't check Slack or email, despite the temptations.

When I'm done writing for the day, I prepare for the next day by reading the upcoming scene beats and encouraging my brain to start working out the story problems I'll be tackling in the morning.

If you're self-publishing, and you probably are if you're reading this, you'll want to do all those other niggling tasks: writing emails, drooling over premade covers, talking to your writer buddies outside of your Maker Time.

You will be able to create your own system based on your circumstances. But the elements of your system should include when you write, how long you write, your ritual before writing, hacks while writing, and how you finish to best prep for the next day.

We'll hit a lot of this in the next couple chapters, but keep in mind that you will be developing a system and then adjusting it as you learn through practice what helps you write fast.

There is a gremlin to be aware of, a demon that can destroy everything you're trying to build. But we can't allow that. So next, let's talk about how to slay your inner editor.

7

TURNING OFF YOUR INNER EDITOR

Turning off your inner editor is vital to writing fast.

If you can't do this, then you're cooking with curdled cream, running with a sprained ankle, or driving a car without any oil. And at some point, there will be a disaster. Your recipe will be ruined, you'll be huffing and puffing as you recover on the side of the road, or you'll have to pull over and your hood raised as dark smoke plumes from engine.

The same is true for your writing, so you need to know that ahead of time and nurture a personal culture that refuses to allow your critical self to stand in the way. If you are judging your work at the same time you're trying to create it, your speed will be hampered along with your overall levels of creativity.

It's vital to figure this out ahead of time and not while you're in the middle of your draft.

Imagine you were about to try a long jump, but instead of leaning into your momentum and going for it, you stopped halfway there to assess how well your thigh muscles are working. Your jump would fail.

Don't let the same thing happen to your writing.

Your inner critic is doing the job it's supposed to do — working to save you from a poorly told story — but it has no business in the actual process of writing.

I'm sure some version of the following sounds familiar.

You started out your story and were really feeling it. Things were going great, and you were excited. But soon enough, whether your insecurity was prompted by something legitimate or simple creative diffidence, you start to see everything as terrible. Your characters are wallpaper, your plot's a leaky bucket, and your premise isn't just garbage, it's long in the tooth and exhausted.

This is a natural evolution, and unless we're delusional, most of us have felt it. Committing our story to the page means we're letting readers into our heads and declaring to the world, *This is what I think a good story looks like.*

The fear can be palpable.

What if it isn't a good story?

What if you don't even know how to write a decent sentence?

What if people hate your writing or think your story is terrible?

You might not be able to turn that inner editor off, but you can learn to ignore it.

Unfortunately, you can't just decide and wait for it to happen. That's what derails a lot of writers. Instead, you need to change the way you think.

Some storytellers don't bother turning off their inner critic because they think they can't. Over time, they've trained themselves to judge and write concurrently because they wrongly see this as a timesaver.

If I get the words perfect in the rough draft, I'll save a bunch of time in the edits!

First of all, your words will *never* be perfect in the draft. That's not how this works. But more importantly (and this is a lesson that's a lot harder to learn), you'll never save time by scrutinizing every sentence while you're trying to *create* the story.

Creation and construction are not synonyms; they are orders of operation.

Your writing will get cleaner over time, but only through consistent practice and letting your words flow. Stopping to think is more likely to turn your writing into something stilted and awkward. It's a process littered with speed bumps instead of the open road that will get your reader looking for more of your work.

There is no automatic kill-switch for your internal critic. A lot of writing fast comes down to having an emotional wrestling match with yourself, over and over again. You won't win every battle, but you'll feel victory for a few, and that will be enough to make you want to polish your armor and head out again, even as it gets beaten and battered.

Sometimes it helps to treat the inner critic like one of those Chinese finger traps you may have gotten stuck in as a child. If you pull against it and try to force it away, it only squeezes tighter. Move toward it, and it releases its hold.

Neeve likes to tell herself, *Yep, I agree. This is a steaming pile of shit. And it's all going to get fixed in the next pass.*

This acknowledges the inner editor instead of trying to stifle it, lets it know it's still protecting you.

It calms down when it knows it doesn't *need* to tell you how crap everything is. There will be a time and place for that.

The first step is to know you're going to write a vomit draft. You're getting the story out because you're smart enough to know how much more you can do with it once the narrative is living outside of your head.

Get down with your adverbs and adjectives, have a party with misplaced punctuation, pretentious word choices, and purple prose. Kill it all later.

Writing quickly — uncensored and with abandon — then clearing the clutter in the aftermath of your draft will turn you into a better writer, faster. During the rewrite, recognizing what sucks then cleaning it up means you've cultivated an eye and can do better the next time.

It also helps to change your goal or reframe your objective.

Yes, you want to write fast. That's why you're here. If there was a button you could click to instantly absorb the ability to write faster than a speeding bullet while hitting a storytelling bulls-eye every time, you would probably click it no matter how much it cost. But that isn't how this works. Only repeated exercise is going to make you stronger here.

So, understand your *actual goal.*

You don't want to write fast, you want to increase your current speed.

Then you want to do that over and over and over again.

Our brains respond positively to stated goals, so declare yours loud and clear, even if it's only to yourself. What are you hitting per hour right now? Do you want to double, triple, or 10X it?

Know your ultimate goal, but decide on something achievable first.

If you write 400 words an hour every hour right now, but you want to write 2,000 eventually, your goal shouldn't be 2,000 words per hour to start, it should be 500 at the most. But 410 is also perfectly legitimate. Once you can hit that every time without fail, you can escalate your goal.

Take the perfectionist side of you that's trying to write a good first draft and make sure it understands that a *perfect* first draft means 1,000 words a day (or whatever is the right number for you). Changing your desired outcome will keep you from judging the individual words and help you focus on their cumulative impact.

Much of what you write while learning to work

faster will not be as good as you want. Especially at first.

That's why you can never, ever forget writing is *rewriting*.

There are at least three stages to every draft: Say it. Say what you mean. Say it well.

Your inner editor doesn't belong in any of them.

Let's look at how to approach those stages so that you can truly calm that inner editor down and start writing fast.

8

TAKE A PASS

REMEMBER, writing fast is about how you see writing. Sometimes the best way to change your thinking around a topic is to adjust your language.

One concept that has helped our storytellers is passes.

Instead of writing a draft, tell yourself you are taking a pass through your manuscript. A draft is a noun. A complete thing in and of itself. When writing a draft, you will naturally want it to be the best version of your story it can possibly be.

Passing through your manuscript is a verb. It's an action. It's easier to see it as a stage of your writing process rather than the end goal. Each time you pass through the manuscript, you hold a specific intention for the pass. This keeps you in one mental state, focused on one outcome. And it does wonders for dimming the inner editor.

You can set your passes however you want, but what follows is how we lay them out.

————

OUTLINE PASSES

The outline is not just one pass. You'll have a brain dump usually followed by a pass where you start to put your elements in order. Then you'll pass back through adding more detail to your beats. If you're working with a partner, you might pass it back and forth, each person adding to the outline until you feel you know your story and it's just dying for life.

————

VOMIT PASS (SAY it)

The vomit pass is what we're focused on when we think about writing fast. It's spewing the words in your head onto a page so you can mold and shape your story into the amazing piece of fiction you know it can be.

Some writers call this the shitty first draft, but

again, that's a static way to see it. Plus, I don't know any storyteller that doesn't secretly want their first draft to be better.

You can vomit a fantastic pass. The more you do this, the better your initial passes will be. It's about the act of getting the words onto the page, not getting them perfectly right.

————

REWRITE Pass (Say What You Mean)

The second pass through your manuscript is where you will start to see the story take shape. Here you're looking at what actually came out and starting to move the pieces around, adding the bits you needed to research, and making sure the story coalesces as a whole.

When you first start focusing on speed, this pass may take longer and feel more laborious. *It should.* But every time you do a rewrite pass you will learn more about how you tell stories.

Soak it in. Feed your subconscious mind and it will only help you write better in your next story.

This pass is important not just for shaping your narrative, but for shaping you as a storyteller.

————

EDIT PASS (SAY it Well)

Now you can look at those crappy sentence structures.

Kill your darlings.

Kick those adjectives out on their asses.

You have a story that makes sense structurally, so now's the time to make it shine.

Don't fall into the habit of spending too much time here, though. You need to nurture the natural voice and flow that came out in your vomit draft.

This process is about looking for stumbling blocks. Look for sentences and word choices that stop your reader from the best possible experience.

————

POLISH PASS

The purpose of this pass is to get your best honest effort to the editor. The quality of your polish passes should constantly improve — a lot at first, then a little over time.

Catch the typos, make a final decision about your Oxford commas, and italicize your inner dialogue.

Giving an editor your best work helps them to move your manuscript from good to great. If they spend all their energy on your typos instead of looking for opportunities to improve word choice or metaphor, you will ultimately get a diminished product and grow less as a storyteller.

As you get better, you may do away with this pass altogether. Many authors do. I still prefer this third pass and want everything I work on to have it. I've experienced surprises in that third pass one-hundred percent of the time, so to me, it's worth exploring. That last pass is also the most fun for me, as I really get to enjoy the story.

I encourage all storytellers to do this pass, but it's more important to do what works for *you*.

———

As YOU SIT for your various passes, it's helpful to remember that it is just that, a pass. It's not writing an epic novel or even a shitty first draft. It's moving what's in front of you forward. It's doing what's right and putting your brain in the proper place to handle the task at hand.

If it helps, write WRITING IS REWRITING on a

PostIt then stick it to your monitor. Give yourself and your inner editor the gift of knowing exactly what each pass is so you can stay focused and actually enjoy your work.

Now, are ready to write?

PART III

LET'S WRITE

9

BEFORE GETTING STARTED

IT'S TIME TO WRITE.

Not necessarily *fast,* but *faster* than you ever have before.

It's not enough to "just start writing." You need to know where you're going and how to get there. First, let's cover a few things you will want to consider before getting started.

The consistency of your schedule is the protein in this meal. You're trying to get stronger, that means you need the habits to support your growth. Never set goals you can't keep.

If you were trying to lose weight because you've been eating poorly for too long and you haven't been to the gym in years, it would be a bad idea to make a goal like, *I'll go to the gym every day for the next month and lose at least twenty-five pounds.*

Going to the gym is hard, and a lot harder if you've not gone in years. By day three, you'll want a break. By day six, you'll be starving for one. By day nine, you'll be dying for it.

You tell yourself one day off won't hurt, and you take it. But it does hurt. You've tarnished the original goal, and your brain knows it. People have control over their behavior in a way they do not have control over a number on their scale.

Don't calculate your odds of success on elements you hold little to no authority over.

A better goal for the above scenario would be, *I'll go to the gym at least once a week for the next six months, be mindful of what I eat without being obnoxious, and measure my results every Sunday night to see where I can improve.*

The second goal will lead to better results for most people a majority of the time. Why? Because it's immediately doable and is sustainable. Also, it gives the person trying to lose weight the ability to see results quickly and become even more successful over time.

And so it goes with writing.

Set yourself up for success.

Get your mind right. You can't just open your office, sit at your desk, then expect the genius to poor out. It doesn't work that way. Never has, never will. Or maybe AI will write our stories for us soon and this is all a waste of time. But for now, you need to show up and be ready to write. What that means is different for everyone, but the key is to train your mind that when it's time to write, *it's time to write.*

You want to build those habits so you're writing with automaticity rather than effort. This starts by establishing an environment that's the same each time you sit to write. Your brain will slip into writing mode as soon as it gets those signals you've setup.

Some people like white noise. Johnny and Dave both enjoy music. They listen to it loud and with lyrics. I'm jealous. I can listen to music, but I'm usually best with classical. Most of the time I prefer silence. But if I'm feeling unmotivated or in any way distracted, I use Brain FM for simple binaural beats to help me stay focused.

One hack that's been responsible for dragging me back from the worst of my procrastination and into right into fluid productivity is a single piece of music that trains you to behave like Pavlov's dog salivating at the sound of a scientist's bell. Results won't be immediate, and the first few times will still be a grind, but once you've trained yourself that a particular piece of music gets you going, writing is much more likely to happen, no matter how reluctant it might be.

Your welcome to borrow my piece of music if you'd like. It's *Rhapsody in Blue*. I love the music itself, but I also have warm feelings of the piece from watching *Fantasia 2000* with my children when they were small. The orchestration has a building, propulsive force and no lyrics to distract me. I use this for editing more than anything else. When I have something I flat out don't want to edit, this piece gets my fingers moving.

Neeve has created a playlist of her favorite writing songs (heavy dubstep that's light on lyrics; yes, I think she's crazy) on Spotify. Getting into writing mode for her is as simple as turning to the playlist and hitting shuffle. Her brain knows it's time to write.

Establish you're writing space. Some storytellers can write with their families around them and others need absolute quiet. Some writers love the feel and sounds and scents of a coffee shop. Preferences change. I used to be able to write anywhere at any time. Now I'm almost belligerent about writing first thing in the morning in solitude.

Your writing space is not just about where you write, it's about how you write. Some of our storytellers write their first draft by hand then type in their words as part of their rewrite pass. Neeve prefers the loudest, clackiest keyboard she can find. She swears the sound of her fingers typing fast puts her in a hypnotic state and knocks her brain right into flow. A few of our storytellers love the Alphsmart Neo, it's become a "thing" in the studio. You can't even buy these things anymore, you have to get them on eBay. But they type away faithfully on the small machine then let it transcribe into their computers later.

There is no right answer beyond the one that works for you — the one it will be easiest for you to treat with consistency. As with mindset, this is all about training your brain to move in a way that keeps your fingers flying.

Don't be afraid of rituals or anything that will help you feel mentally and emotionally prepared to write. It's work. Just because you will be sitting or standing at the keyboard doesn't mean you're not taxing yourself as much as someone working retail or running a company. Whether that means having your first cup of coffee, going for a walk, or getting into downward dog before opening your story for the day, build yourself a trigger. Think of an action you can do as a precursor to the kind of writing day you want to have.

I make coffee every morning. I usually have just the one cup for the entire day and use it more as a trigger to start my writing than I do for the caffeine. If you already have a habit you love and never miss, then linking it to your creative discipline might be a smart cut to making it routine.

We talked about planning already, but it bears repeating: the importance of your pre-writing routine and its correlation to writing fast can't be stressed enough. Before starting, you must absolutely know your story and your purpose.

You need a solid idea of what you want to say. Not every note, but at the very least a through line, how the characters are going to fill it, and what the world is like around them. Finer details can and should come while you're writing the story, but if you expect it all to happen in the narrative, you'll spend an awful lot of time staring at the screen waiting for it to show up.

If you're writing nonfiction, your purpose is simple. It's the problem you're trying to solve. But if you're writing fiction, you need at least a loose idea of the feeling you want your reader to have when she's finished with the book.

I always do better when I have a mood in mind for a scene. For Johnny, mood often comes first, and that's one of the things that helps him crank out quality copy across so many genres. The details come because he's fluent in the mood, and that temperament makes it easier for us to design our reader experience.

Your purpose can change through the draft. In a good book, it will organically grow. But starting with a loose idea will help you write with speed and precision.

Go over your beats, outline, or scene before you sit down to write. You can even look at it before your trigger (like getting that first cup of coffee) so it can play through your mind as you prepare.

This will help it all fly out when you sit to write.

10

NOW WRITE!

OKAY, NOW it's time to write!

You're in the perfect environment. You know the story you want to tell. The conditions are right, and you're ready with your plot and purpose in mind. Your inner editor has gone fishing and your headphones are on.

Start writing and don't stop.

Keep going, no matter what.

If you need to pause for a moment because something requires thought, be aware of how long it's taking. You can easily spend ten minutes pondering something unimportant that you could do a better job with in thirty seconds in the next pass. You'll know more than you do now and be in a different state of mind. Your job in the first vomit pass isn't to figure every little thing out. It's to tell yourself the first version of the story. If you don't know the details, leave them for your future self to figure out. It's a favor to both of you.

Use a placeholder for anything that requires thought for later.

If your hero is about to step into some sprawling fantasy land and you want it to be an epic display of your imagination and craftsmanship, fine. Save it for later. This is a place where it would be easy for an author to trade an hour for a handful of words when something like EPIC DESCRIPTION HERE would do for now. Because the point of the scene isn't to cast the spell the reader will feel when experiencing this world for the first time, and the hero really needs to meet the heroine who is waiting on the other side of this particular veil.

If *you* need that description to get where you need to go, then by all means explore it. But be aware of your time. Writing faster will require you to surrender some of your instincts. Don't skip the epic description just because but hop over it if it's holding you back. If it's flowing out of you, great. If not, leave a note for yourself to fill it in only after you've turned on your thinking mind later. Right now, you're writing.

The same goes for research. If you're the type of writer who will turn away from drafting to look something up then lose an hour down a rabbit hole of research, you have to stop that. Make a decision. You're probably telling yourself a book can't be written that way. You need to color in the lines as you go. But try it a different way and see how it works for you. Many authors protest this, not wanting to leave gaps in their draft to constantly move forward, but I've yet to meet one who gave it their all and saw no results.

If you have a difficult time even trying this, find an app or Internet blocker to keep you offline. You can fill in the details when you switch it on later.

Maybe a new character shows up and you didn't expect it. Names are important to you, a part of your character building that normally gets a lot of your thought. Stopping your flow to name that character in the middle of your writing session is a terrible idea. You can name them ABC or XYZ or Madam Consuela. Just come back after your writing session to name your characters. When you're preparing for the coming day is the perfect time to start thinking about it.

Come up with a way to easily find these gaps in your writing by making your notation system consistent. Try using a symbol you don't normally use in writing then use the search function to make sure you don't miss a single one. If you're using Scrivener or StoryShop, your notes can be added as an inline comment to yourself, making them very easy to find.

We (embarrassingly) recently published a book with XYZ city and never filled it in. Having a particular way of noting this will help you to have peace of mind that this won't happen to you.

The number one thing that will hold you back in the writing phase, especially if you're trying to do it fast, is a failure to feel excited about your work. If you're not pleased to be writing *and* you're doing it fast, I feel sorry for your editor, and maybe even your eventual readers.

If you know your story, are excited to tell it, and think writing slow is only something you do because you haven't yet figured out a better way to do things, then you shouldn't let anything hold you back from your writing.

Beyond the obstacles standing in the way of writing flow are the things you want to lean into. Knowing who you are and operating around your tendencies is the most organic way to optimize results. Especially the kind that are easier to maintain. This isn't just knowing your habits away from the page, but getting more in touch with who you are as a writer.

Do you write action better than anything else?

Do you FLY when it's time for some fast-paced dialogue?

Do you live to write sprawling monologues that go on and on?

Pay attention to the areas in your draft that keep you writing fast, and use that as a way to increase your speed over time. They'll increase your quality, too, since the elements you're naturally faster at are also the ones you're probably better at. By structuring future stories around what you write best, the words will come faster and be more likely to resonate with your readers.

And remember, the slower stuff can always be filled in the next pass. Bonnie almost never adds full location descriptions on her first pass. She loves the action. She'll go back and fill in the details that bring her scene to life on a rewrite pass. Without this adjustment to her comfort zone, Bonnie would never be able to write nearly as much as she wants to.

It's been said, but you're writing now so you cannot forget it, no matter what:

Focus is everything.

A flow state will help you write in a state of

hypnosis, letting it pour forth from your subconscious. Getting there will never happen by accident. Yes, you want to block the usual distractions — go to a different room, close the door, put your phone on Do Not Disturb.

But that's only the beginning.

Self-awareness is everything. Pay attention to what you're doing. If your mind starts to wander, usher it back to where it's supposed to go. If you feel yourself falling into negative patterns of thought, give yourself some of the self-talk that will send your thinking in the opposite direction.

Take regular breaks. Writing fast requires you to work your mind harder than it might be used to. A walk around the block can help you to reset it.

Don't make the mistake of thinking you can actually multi-task. Writing is writing, don't pair it with anything else. You can't be on social media and write or have a TV on in the background. If you want to write fast and well, you must be disciplined in what you're offering the process.

Train yourself to get stronger. If you can write in a flurry for fifteen minutes, excellent. Try twenty, thirty, forty-five, an hour.

Learn to trust the process. Your instincts will get incrementally sharper every time you write. My process is a lot different from what it was years ago, but that's mostly because that's now one of my golden rules. It's not just easier to trust the process than it was before our studio had a few hundred books behind us, it's now impossible to approach it any other way.

In the beginning, we didn't yet have all this experience to draw on, but we could still see every project got easier to do. We were always able to dream bigger than the last time, only because of what we had managed to pull off before.

Write, don't think.

It's remarkable how often I'll go back and read something I've previously written and find it surprising. Not just a line here or there, but full pages, and sometimes not long after I've finished them.

Focus gets you there. You're writing fast enough to mainline the story. Tapped into it deep enough that your subconscious starts doing most of the work. You know your characters and your plot. You're confident about your surroundings. The words come as an immediate extension of thought.

This is bliss for a writer. And for the editor.

My fastest copy is the easiest to edit for others, and the same is true for Dave and Johnny. The faster their copy was written, the cleaner it's likely to be.

This only comes from experience. You will probably be surprised by how good some of your speed writing is, but don't be discouraged if it's not yet where you want it to be.

Remember, *faster* not *fast.*

Next, let's talk about some of the hacks we use to get there.

11

TRICKS WE USE TO GO FAST

A LOT of writing faster comes down to tricking your-self into doing better.

Google *tricks to write faster* and you'll find enough links to keep you busy and not writing for a year. If you don't find what you're looking for in this book, please find a method that feels like it might work for you and keep experimenting until something clicks. But after well over a century of our studio's collective experience, these are the five tricks we use to consistently write faster.

———

SPRINTS

Placing a boundary around your writing will

help you to achieve focus faster. Let's say you've been setting aside an hour each day to write. Unfortunately, you're getting barely any words in that time. You start out strong, with a couple hundred or so, but then you peter out.

Pay attention to what's happening. Instead of an hour block, you find that a fifteen-minute sprint gives you eighty percent of the words you were able to get if given the full hour you've just proven you don't need. What if you could divide your day differently, and get four fifteen-minute sprints instead, or three for twenty-minutes each? How about a pair of half-hours?

You can focus on anything for fifteen minutes. But if you find yourself checking your phone twenty-seven minutes into the sprint, you might not have the muscle. You need time to build it.

Take a breather between sprints. If you still have the full hour and you want to work in a single block, you'll still probably find that you're getting more words in three fifteen-minute sprints with a five-minute break between each than you did in a full, uninterrupted hour.

Don't switch to another task and hurl your brain into something else. Make your rest meaningful. Walk away from the story for a few minutes to genuinely reset. This could be getting up and stretching, looking out a window to let your eyes focus on a farther point, doing jumping jacks, or even jumping on a rebounder.

Sprints help you to assess how you're doing. You can keep track of your per sprint word count. You're not competing with others; you're competing with yourself. Tallying the small wins will keep you going when doing so might otherwise be difficult.

We'll talk about streaks in the full *Momentum* book, but it's the combination of streaks and sprints that makes me as productive as I am. Those two elements are probably responsible for eighty-percent of my productivity.

The rest of these tricks are possible because of our studio, but there is an individual variant for each.

―――――

THE DAILY FUCK *Yeah*

This was born when Joel asked the studio for a much-needed ass-kicking. He knew he was capable of hitting several thousand words a day, but it just wasn't happening. He kept promising himself and us he would, yet he kept repeatedly coming short of his personal expectations. After talking it out as a group, we realized Joel just needed some daily accountability.

If he had a place to report his daily words, that might make all the difference in the world. And it did. Immediately. Joel increased his average by a factor of ten, going from writing a few hundred words a day to over thirty-five hundred.

The Daily Fuck Yeah is a Slack channel where we post the number we hit each day. The storytellers cheer each other on no matter what the number is.

Even more amazing, this had a company-wide effect. With everyone dropping their words into a collective count, the entire studio started piling syllables higher. Our total count rose over twenty-percent across the board. The effect was immediate, and the growth has held. We have some writers making cheese and others who proudly share their counts, even on insane days that only moved their draft forward by twenty-three words. It's all celebrated, so all of it matters.

You don't need a studio, but if you find one person to cheer you on and report to daily, the extra touchpoint and accountability will keep you more consistent.

———————

Making Cheese

There's a lot of special phrases around Sterling & Stone. The place is totally roosters.

Phrases are born then bandied about, and sometimes they stick. Like roosters, *making cheese* is here to stay.

It all started one Saturday when Johnny posted in Slack, "I assume everyone else is making cheese today, too."

A flurry of responses followed. The storytellers didn't know if he meant actual cheese, writing extra fast, or something dirty. He came back an hour later to discover a lot of wild ideas about making cheese. It turned out Johnny was making cheese with his daughter, Sydney. Literally making cheese, the food. He wasn't writing or doing anything else non-dairy related. He posted a picture to prove it.

We all agreed it was significant, and we declared that henceforth writing ten-thousand words in a day would be called "making cheese."

Now this is like the ringing of a bell. We live to make cheese. When somebody posts 10,000 or more in the DailyFuckYeah, it's usually answered with a bunch of cheese wedge emojis.

This is another simple tweak that's led to a nice little studio growth spurt. Appropriately enough, Johnny was the first to make cheese. And a lot of it. He was running behind on a project and had to catch up. He ended up making cheese for five days in a row to make a book that barely had to be edited. Caitlin made cheese next. I was dying for my turn.

Making cheese became a goal. Not just then, but thereafter.

There have been days when I'm at around eight-thousand words and instead of feeling tired, I get inspired to finish it off and make cheese. Not every storyteller in our studio thought ten-thousand words a day was possible for them, but *making cheese* sounds like a lot more fun.

Our current record holder is Ninie, with a whopping 14,322, which is brie and crackers if you ask her. Ninie didn't know she could even do that before. And that's nothing. Read her finished work and you'll really be blown away.

Johnny just asked me to edit that last part because he was sure he actually has the highest daily word count. He wants the record to state that he holds the actual record at 14,704.

Thanks for taking that away from the studio's surrogate grandma, Johnny.

Create your own saying, or borrow ours and start making cheese. Or at least dream about it.

————

Write-ins.

This was all Marie. She's like a pixie flitting to every part of our studio, paying attention to everything and seeing what might apply to her. She really liked the results of Joel's DailyFuckYeah, and wanted something to keep her writing even harder. Ideally, like the DFY it should help everyone.

So, the write-in was born, and man do our storytellers love them. They all get together in a Zoom room for two hours and write in fifteen-minute sprints with talking in between each one. Sometimes they're discussing their stories and helping each other get unstuck. Sometimes they're telling the amazing (true) story of how they once almost drowned in a dog bowl.

Write-ins are great bonding experiences and will also help you to stay more accountable. It's easier to produce a lot when you're doing it alongside others. If you have no problem getting in two or three sprints per day on your own, it's reasonable to believe you could get in four or five with the support of other writers around you. They'll push you in a way that makes it so you'll want to keep pushing yourself.

Neeve writes fast in her fifteen-minute sprints, but she has trouble keeping herself at the desk to get more sprints in each day. When the DailyFuckYeah started, she was injured and struggling to maintain her normal routine, logging a few hundred words a day. We added write-ins the to the mix, and her count jumped to a few thousand. In the midst of painkiller fog and hospital appointments, she was having a hard time sitting down and writing on her own. She came to the write-ins to see her Sterling & Stone family but ended up doing four or five sprints with the gang.

Don't know of a write-in? Start one. Invite some writers to a weekly session. Show up and do exactly what you said you would do: *write.* Don't worry if there are only a few other writers or even just two of you. That's still enough for the write-in to do everything you need it to do.

———

REWRITE YOUR FIRST CHAPTER.

You don't have to actually rewrite your first chapter, but this is a simple hack I've used for a long time that helps me write fast rather than second-guessing every other sentence (which can easily start to happen if I wander into the wrong mindspace).

First chapters used to take me approximately a million hours. I would start out slow then meander through a lot of throat-clearing. It didn't matter how detailed my beats were because that wasn't the problem. Until I learned the world around me and had a feeling for its mood, it felt more like I was making things up as I went along than telling the story that had to be told. The difference between them equals the polarity between frustration and flow.

The fix was simple. I changed the way I thought about starting my books and eliminated the problem. I reminded myself that I could always rewrite the first chapter, and that maybe I even should. You never know your characters when you're starting, at least not like you will later. Same for your world or your rhythm or anything else that's unique to that particular story.

I started rewriting my first chapter as soon as I finished the last. I don't always do this now, but I always know I can, and that knowledge stays with me as I work my way through the draft. Your *first chapter* really means *any chapter*.

———

ADD your own tricks and hacks. We call ours out and give them a name because the act of deciding what you will do to help you write faster often helps you hold yourself to a higher standard.

Now that you're writing and have a system and environment (plus a few tricks to keep you there), it's time to help you stay there.

PART IV

DODGING PITFALLS

12

WHEN WRITING GOES AWRY

DESPITE ALL YOUR BEST PLANS, sometimes writing simply isn't going to happen for you. This is an omnipresent possibility, so don't be surprised. Instead, it's helpful to fall back on your tools and goals to get yourself back in the game.

———

FIRST, Examine Your Thinking

Have you fallen back into your old mental habits? Are you staring off into space trying to come up with the perfect sentence instead of just vomiting it out?

It's okay if you have, it happens. Bring yourself

back to the space — without any mental berating, please. And continue.

One thing that helps is to refocus on your current goal. Are you on the vomit pass? If so, the purpose is to just get words on the paper. It can and will be molded into a story later. That's not the objective right now.

————

ARE YOU DISTRACTED?

Sometimes the worst distractions are rattling around between your ears. All the ones we've already discussed, like your inner editor berating your every mistake, but also any personal stuff you might be going through. Right now, my parents are being awful and it's constantly in my head. I can't allow an unfortunate truth to interfere with my work, nor can I pretend it doesn't exist. This has been going on for a few days, and it has significantly affected my word count. But I didn't let that happen today. I wrote a thousand words to myself, getting my parents out of my head so I could get on with my day.

That may seem counterintuitive, writing outside of my work in progress while trying to go fast. But this book was designed to be written fast. Originally, I wanted to make cheese (write more than 10,000 words in a day) to finish each part of this book in one day.

But that didn't happen.

Yesterday, despite spending a full writing day on the project, I hit only half of my goal.

I could have repeated history today and ended up with half of my word count again, for better or worse. Instead, I got that thousand for me out of the way so I could get in another nine-thousand for you. And clearing my head didn't just make the writing more fluid, it gave me a much better day.

Swab the decks as much as you can. You're a writer, so use writing as an exercise to usher in clarity. If you're distracted by life, write it out. Get the words down. Pull the thoughts out of your head so your brain can relax, knowing you've done something to address your worries and concerns.

Now you have the mental space to return to your project.

———

Fall Back on Tools

I've given you a lot of tools in this book so far.

Use them. When something goes wrong, it's often because you've gone out of your system or are trying to make your brain work in two modes at once. This can happen at any stage of a project.

My struggle in this project was an issue in my personal life, Neeve's was fear. We'll talk more about limiting beliefs and fear in a moment. But let's look at how Neeve used the tools to emerge from her rewriting funk.

Neeve and I passed the outline of this book back and forth a few times until it was ready to write. I did the vomit pass (is that grossing you out yet?), then Neeve did the first rewrite to shape what I'd given her. That's when she got stuck.

My words flowed well because I wrote fast and in that fugue state where my best work comes from. She could see points that should be added and bits in need of some clarity, but she was struggling with where to put her words in a way that wouldn't interrupt the existing rhythm. Ultimately, it all came down to a fear of messing everything up.

Then, of course, she remembered she was writing a book about going fast and she had many tools to fall back on.

First, she separated out the "deciding and the doing." Neeve did a fast pass leaving notes to herself on the side about what she thought needed to be added or changed. Then she did a second pass through, adding content based on those notes. It meant on her first pass, she did the deciding without having to worry about the actual words. On the second pass, she could put her brain into writing mode and add the words she knew were needed.

During the passes, she also used those tricks we talked about to help get her brain focused and not thinking about her fears. She set a timer and worked in fifteen-minute sprints. (Neeve downloaded an alert tone that was the sound of a crowd applauding, because who doesn't need a bit of cheering on as they work?) She set up Spotify to her favorite dubstep playlist and plowed through.

This was all in a rewrite pass, but the same thing can hit at any stage of your work. When you get stuck, do a quick mental assessment, make a new system to move you forward, and keep going.

13

LIMITING BELIEFS THAT KEEP YOU FROM GETTING FASTER

WE WANT to keep you clear of the danger zones, and there's nothing more hazardous to your success than the sort of limiting beliefs that will obstruct your efforts by wrongly convincing you of what you cannot do.

Let's start with *fast writing is poor writing.*

You've met Ninie. She writes faster than just about anybody in the studio (yes, Johnny, you still hold the record). She has several thousand reviews. Her average is 4.8 stars, and Ninie's audience *loves* her.

I used Ninie, but that's true across our studio. Quality always comes before revenue.

But you don't have to take our word for it. Maybe you even think our stories are garbage and nothing like what you want to write. Or that it's easy to talk about writing fast when the tools have never been better.

Not a bit of that matters.

Let's talk about Robert Heinlein. His books have sold well, endured over time, and he had none of our modern implements of creative convenience. He still believed writing raw and fast was the best way to capture passion. He still felt rewriting was practically a sin. Look at how simple his rules were, and how well they still hold up today.

———

1. You must write.

2. You must finish what you write.

3. You must refrain from rewriting, except to editorial order.

4. You must put the work on the market.

5. You must keep the work on the market until it is sold.

———

WRITE, publish, repeat says it a bit more concisely,

and gives it a warm and fuzzy circle of life vibe, but the message is mostly the same.

But we do diverge from Robert's third point — that you should never rewrite, or barely at all. That worked writing science for pulp magazines in the Stone Age, but it would be career suicide now.

Writing is rewriting. But that has nothing to do with the first pass.

If you're laboring under the limiting belief that writing fast will dilute the quality of your work, please divorce yourself of any connection between the rough draft and your finished story. They are siblings, not twins.

Understand the world has changed. The biggest authors used to publish one book a year, if they were prolific. But Stephen King today would be just another guy. That paradigm is done, built on an old model that doesn't make any sense. The practice of spacing an author's books at least one year apart is an old idea, crafted when one-hundred percent of published books required a print run.

The old way has died. We don't yet know what it will turn into, but we do know it's a great time to be a storyteller, especially if you shed the old limiting belief that authors are competing for shelf space. The competition is there, but different than it used to be, driven by the same must-know-now impulse that fuels binge viewing today. When Netflix started releasing their seasonal shows with every episode available, binge viewing became an even bigger thing and forever changed consumer expectations for entertainment \. Shortly after that, the *New York Times* reported that the "ideal" is now for authors to release books in a series every three months.

Writers love to buy books about how to get better or more productive at the craft, exactly like this one. But they don't always implement what they're learning, especially not at the accelerated pace required to move fast and maintain your momentum. Too many writers fail to understand that learning is doing. There will never be a substitute for turning the wheel of your craft around and around and around until it finally starts turning itself.

Every writer in our studio is actively writing, every day, and that makes all the difference in the world. Because their eyes are always inside their story, they're staying in flow, keeping curious, and constantly sharing what they are learning to help the rest of us grow.

You don't need a studio or collaborators to benefit from this lesson. You should read craft books, absolutely. I read less than I used to, but I still read several every year. But my work is a much better teacher. So is sharing with my team. Learn by doing, and share as often as you can.

Lastly, get the phrase *I can't do it* out of your head.

You're this deep into the book, so obviously you *want* to write fast. And we want to see that happen for you. But if you're saying or thinking *I can't,* then you are telling yourself that truth and part of you is believing it. That makes the work a lot harder than it needs to be.

We've seen the results more times than we can count. A lot more times than we can count. Up close and far away. We're constantly getting emails from writers giving us the credit for 10xing their writing. We don't deserve it. There's a ton of writing advice out there. If someone writes significantly faster, it's because they've done the work.

We've seen it happen for every writer in our studio, including Dave. It's summer, and he's already done more this year than in the last two put together.

If we all did it, you can, too.

14

COMMON PITFALLS THAT KEEP YOU FROM WRITING FAST (AND OVERCOMING WRITER'S BLOCK)

YOUR LIMITING beliefs are dealt with. By the end of this section, we're going to clear the rest of the bigger potential obstacles that might stand in the way of flow. You can get blocked, but that doesn't mean there is such a thing as *writer's block*. People get stuck. That's a human thing, not exclusive to storytellers. Giving it the name writer's block makes it sound like an acceptable part of the process.

But writer's block should be something to avoid at all costs, not anything considered *part of the process.*

You can avoid most of these common pitfalls by being aware of them and having a strategy ready to go.

———

You Can't Come Up With an Idea

This sucks. We have ALL been here. We're staring at a blank page, typing and deleting and typing and deleting and typing and OH MY GAWD!!!! we want to scream.

Maybe we can find some inspiration on YouTube.

Almost for sure we can do that.

But we can't get more than a paragraph written because we have no idea what to write about. No idea what story we're even supposed to be telling right now.

We've crashed into a brick wall many miles from home.

None of that is true for me anymore, and it shouldn't be for you.

You're smarter than that. You understand ideas are cheap — way cheaper than most people realize — and you only need one to get you going to the next. Just keep generating new ones. Don't question whether those ideas are good enough, use each one as a rung to grab another. Start climbing, and more often than not, you'll have too many. Instead of trying to find the perfect idea, you're getting your brain back into the practice of idea-making. Don't stare into space looking for ONE idea, write down twenty, then see which one jumps out as something that actually works for you.

It's a different problem if you have a ton of ideas but can't commit to any of them. They're all exciting at the start, but everything sort of fizzles out before you can get it to launch.

This is a more difficult problem, but you still want to start in the same place, by identifying the issue.

Have you lost interest in your idea after a few paragraphs because the character doesn't compel you? Do you have a short story when you thought you had a novel? Those are the kinds of problems that should be caught in the planning phase. If you haven't connected with your character during the outline phase you're going to have a harder time writing fast. Same if you haven't drawn out the story to determine its relative level of depth. But if your problem is simply that you don't know where to take your story next, then take it *somewhere.*

Sometimes super cool ideas fizzle fast and dumb ideas go in places you never expect. Writing fast doesn't allow for you to meander in between. It demands you to be willing to stick with an idea and see where it goes, no matter what, because the movement of your brain is what matters most of all.

Problems don't always appear for the first time in your draft. If you're having trouble getting through your draft because of a problem with the outline, you will almost for sure have difficulty achieving speed or velocity. At least if you're wanting clean words and clarity of story. The solution here is to know what kind of writer you are. Do you want a straight line to your destination or a few points on the map to follow?

Knowing your needs will help you assemble the elements required to achieve your momentum and ensure steady progress isn't impeded. Ask yourself a series of questions to diagnose your outline.

Does it have a major flaw that you're working hard to avoid? Are you trying not to look it in the eye because doing so might fill you with doubts about the entire endeavor?

Is it keeping you from reaching your destination because there's a roadblock of logic right in the middle that doesn't make any sense? You've told yourself there's a way around the lunacy, but you're wasting an awful lot of time looking for it?

A broken outline is a difficult thing to write through. In this instance, it's a good idea to take a break from your story to attack the outline or plan directly.

If your outline isn't the problem but you're still feeling blocked, it's worth stepping away from the project, anyway. If there's a part of your story you can't muscle through and really feels like a slog, you need to know *why*. Even if that doesn't help you to go faster now, it may help you go faster on every project going forward. Maybe your story is boring in that spot or you have your characters doing things they wouldn't actually do. It's an artifact from your time as god of the overall story, before you knew the people you would be writing about. Those characters might be your best lead in figuring out where to go next.

Try free writing about your story instead of working on the story itself. This can eliminate some of the mental pressure of getting it right and put you back into the mode of playing with the story and the characters. That more relaxed writing can help you find the direction you want to go next with the story.

Take a detour, go off on a tangent, see where the story takes you. It's quite possible — it happens to us all the time — that you'll find a much cooler transition between one moment to the next and that will help you to figure out where to take your story. Don't worry if there are irrelevant elements here. They can be cut later. Remember, the fast draft is about getting it down.

Maybe your gut says your story took a wrong turn and now you've hit a dead end.

You don't know what to do, and that rampart in front of you makes you feel like turning around and giving up. You were trying to do something bold, maybe even clever, but it didn't work out, and now that couple of degrees you started flying off course has put you thousands of miles away from your destination.

If you're certain you've gone the wrong way, then there's no point in going forward. Doing so will only worsen the problem. Assess instead. Then make the best possible choice.

You can either keep going and leave yourself holes to plug later, or you can partially rewind, returning to a place in your story that still makes sense and hasn't gone astray. If writing fast is your goal, then you always want to err on the side of momentum. Make the decision that will give you thrust without putting your narrative in jeopardy.

Either way, you will end up with two alternate time-lines to track during the revision. Be aware, but don't let work that must be done later interfere with your job in the present.

I closed last year writing a trilogy with Dave. Two-thirds through the second book, I realized that I'd strayed too far from my beats. Totally my fault. There was nothing wrong with the way Dave had written them, I just wasn't paying enough attention to what was coming and ended up writing myself into a corner.

I had a choice. I could either go back and rewrite three chapters to make everything in the story so far agree with my mistake. Or I could write a new chapter that justified what I had done. I chose the new chapter. Not only did it fix the problem, it made for a better story and provided a much better foundation for the third and final book in that series.

It takes time to develop this level of trust in your story. To know everything will work out if you just keep writing forward. But getting stuck still happens no matter how many books you write, so it's always more important to develop your skillset around knowing what to do when it happens than it is on learning how to avoid it altogether.

The last common pitfall to be especially aware of is a dark headspace you will always want to steer clear of.

Not everyone is going to love your story. No matter how good it is, some readers are going to say it sucks. Look at your favorite books, movies, and TV shows. Go read the reviews. A lot of people hate what you love. That's fine. You're never going to please everyone, and if you're trying to do that while writing the story, you're going to have an incredibly difficult time doing it fast.

Most writer's block boils down to fear.

Fear of putting yourself out there.

Fear of failure if you do.

Fear of success.

Fear of not living up to your personal expectations, a pre-existing standard, your high school English teacher, parents, peers, or whatever.

You need to get out of those dark corners inside your head and into the light. Fear is one of the leading causes of paralysis. Don't let your inner critic participate in the art of creation. Don't think about haters or potential one-star reviews. Odds are excellent that your ideas are better than your darkest fears are whispering. Even if they're not, you'll still have the chance to revise them later, and considering a worst-case scenario while writing will slow you down one hundred percent of the time.

In the raw draft, you want to move fast, so keep the door closed and write only for yourself.

CONCLUSION

WRITING IS A MENTAL ENDEAVOR. Every word you put on the page starts in your brain. Learning to write faster is as simple as learning how to use your brain and use it well.

All the tools, tricks, and ideas in this book help you to do one very simple thing that will make you write faster than anything else: *focus your brain on one thing at a time.*

Planning and passes help you separate out the deciding and doing.

When you plan, you are deciding the kind of story to tell and the guideposts that will take you and your reader on the journey you want to go on. Drawing scenes and details from your life or casting characters gives you permission to fly without having to decide on all the little details as you write.

Passes give your brain a clear delineation between each activity. You're not trying to write and make an amazing novel at the same time. If that's what you've been doing so far, *stop*. It's making you take way longer than you need to and probably having a detrimental effect on your writing.

Remember: *Say it, say what you mean, say it well.*

Always know and stick to the point of your current pass, and your brain will stay more focused than ever before.

We've detailed a lot of tricks and hacks, all of them designed to tell your brain it's time to write then hold it to task.

Sprints keep your mind from wandering. Write-ins and dailyfuckyeahs help your brain stay focused on the goal of daily words instead of writing well. They also offer external accountability. Setting up your routine and writing environment triggers neural pathways in your brain to help you find your flow faster.

Writing fast isn't easy, but it's been achievable for every author we've worked with so far. Remember, you might want to write fast, but this isn't driving and there is no universal speed. Your goal should be writing faster than you did before. Knowing you can do it and committing to making it happen will change the way your brain works. You will write better, get more creative, and learn to live in flow.

One of your biggest goals in reading this book isn't just to *write faster;* you also want to enjoy the craft more than you do. Writing shouldn't feel like a struggle, and you know that. Everything I've told you in this book is useless if you hate the process. You are writing not just as a way to earn money, but because you love the craft. Never sacrifice that love for speed or anything else. You'll probably find that as you go faster, your joy is bolstered alongside your quality.

Storytellers have more fun when they're doing it fast. We hear authors complaining about the grind of writing all the time, but none of those writers is on fire. They are all slow and wish the work felt different than it does. You're tired of feeling that way and are now doing something about it.

Keep your mind open and use the trial of writing fast to know yourself better.

This is a different skill than what you're used to, and learning to do it well will force your growth in the best possible way. Maybe you've never had to plan at this level, kill your inner critic, write without ever going backward, or do it in streaks throughout the day.

You will be consistently challenged, so you must always understand that *if it doesn't challenge you, it cannot change you.*

Acknowledge the challenge on your way to the change. Embrace it as part of the process.

And do everything you can to stay consistent with your discipline.

The more you practice anything, the better you will get at it. Storytelling isn't any different. Write every day to grow every day. You'll not only get faster — if that's one of the elements of your craft you're paying attention to — you will constantly improve.

Writers are infamous procrastinators, but you're better than that. You know that behavior is holding you back. You're doing the little things that will help you develop the habit and stay consistent with it. Maybe you're writing in sprints or reporting into your version of the DailyFuckYeah. Maybe you're using write-ins to stay steady in your intentions, or perhaps you're pouring your efforts into making cheese.

Collaboration isn't for everyone, but best-case scenario, you're smart enough to realize your results will be better if you're not working to achieve them all by yourself. Instead of simply committing to yourself, consider making a promise to an accountability partner. Two people trying to write faster together will always have a better chance at succeeding than one.

There is nothing more important than consistency, and in the full book *Momentum*, you will learn to take your newfound ability to write fast and turn that into a sustainable practice you can build a business around.

For now, remember writing faster is almost always more about what you let go of than the tools you add to your toolbox. It's about quieting your inner critic while you write, letting your doubts and fears fall to the wayside. It's about trusting the process and letting yourself enjoy the act of writing.

You write alone. Even when collaborating. There is nobody there but you and your characters and your story. You should be the first person to enjoy that story. Later, on the next passes, you can rewrite for your audience, for your editor, for the world. But always write for YOU first. Enjoy it, and watch that love of writing grow as you write faster.

Now take this book, apply what you've learned, and write the hell out of your next project.

ACCESS THE VAULT

The best way to retain what you just learned is through reminders and application.

We've created a **60-Second Summary** of the key points in this book for you to print and keep handy as you begin to incorporate what you learned.

You'll find the summary, PLUS *all our extra downloadables for the entire Stone Tablet range* in our Extras Vault.

Visit **SterlingAndStone.net/Extras** to get access.

Lightning Source UK Ltd.
Milton Keynes UK
UKHW011840120120
356820UK00001B/81/P